# BOOM SCIENCE

# PLANTS

Georgia Amson-Bradshaw

# BOOM SCIENCE

# PLANTS

Georgia Amson-Bradshaw

PowerKiDS press

Published in 2020 by The Rosen Publishing Group, Inc.
29 East 21st Street, New York, NY 10010

Cataloging-in-Publication Data

Names: Amson-Bradshaw, Georgia.
Title: Plants / Georgia Amson-Bradshaw.
Description: New York : PowerKids Press, 2020. | Series: Boom science |
Includes glossary and index.
Identifiers: ISBN 9781725303812 (pbk.) | ISBN 9781725303843 (library
bound) | ISBN 9781725303829 (6pack)
Subjects: LCSH: Plants--Juvenile literature.
Classification: LCC QK49.A56 2020 | DDC 581--dc23

Series Editor: Georgia Amson-Bradshaw
Series Designer: Rocket Design (East Anglia) Ltd

Picture acknowledgements:
Images from Shutterstock.com: Tatjana Romanova 7l, Vaclav Volrab 7r,
ANURAKE SINGTO-ON 7br, Nikitina Olga 8, moryachok 9tl, Food_asia 9c,
shubin42 9, Anastasiia 9, Skorobogatova 13t, Christine C Brooks 13l, Gracy
Oliver 13b udaix 14, kc_film 15c, Ian Fletcher 15b, ensiferum 16l, nafanya241
16b, Maria_OH 17t, Anastasiia Skorobogatova 17b, Sergey Chirkov 18b,
Richard Griffin 19, Zerbor 23l, Sanit Fuangnakhon  23, rsooll 23b, luckypic 24t,
DK Arts 24b, Esin Deniz 25b.
All illustrations on pages 10, 11, 20, 21, 26, 27 by Steve Evans

All design elements from Shutterstock.

Manufactured in the United States of America

CPSIA Compliance Information: Batch CSPK19: For Further Information contact Rosen Publishing,
New York, New York at 1-800-237-9932.

Glossary words are shown in bold.

# CONTENTS

# PLANTS

Plants are living things that come in many shapes and sizes.

## BIG, SMALL, HARD, SOFT

There are many different kinds of plant, from tiny cress to giant trees. Cactus plants are hard and spiky. Grass plants are soft and brushy.

Who wants a hug from a cactus?

# WOW!

The tallest tree in the world is a redwood tree. It can be 380 feet (115 m) tall. That's as tall as a skyscraper!

# FLOWER POWER

Most plants have **flowers**. These are called **flowering plants**. Some plants do not have flowers. These are called **nonflowering plants**.

A fern is a nonflowering plant.

A crocus is a flowering plant.

## HEY, WHAT AM I?

What sort of plant is this?
Answer on page 28.

## HIDE AND SEEK

A daisy is a small, white flowering plant. How many can you spot hiding?

# ROOTS AND STEMS

Roots anchor a plant in the ground, and a stem holds it up.

## STRONG STEMS

The **stem** is the part of the plant that supports the **leaves** and flowers. Some stems are very big. A tree's **trunk** is its main stem.

← - - - stem

## HIDING UNDERGROUND

The **roots** are the part of the plant you don't normally see, because they are buried in the soil. They hold the plant firmly in the ground.

roots

**SLURP!**

## THIRSTY LEAVES

Stems have hollow tubes, like straws, inside them. The tubes carry water and **nutrients** from the roots to the leaves and the flowers.

# WOW!

Tree roots are very strong. They can even crack pavement as they grow!

## HAIRY ROOTS

Roots are covered in tiny hairs. The hairs suck up water and nutrients from the soil.

### HEY, WHAT AM I?

What can you see in this picture? Answer on page 28.

# YOUR TURN!

# COLOR CHANGE CELERY

Prove that stems carry water up to the leaves. You'll need:

Three colors of food coloring

A bunch of celery with leaves

Three glasses of water

## STEP ONE

Put a few drops of food coloring into each glass of water and mix. Blue, red, and yellow food coloring work well.

Ask an adult to trim the celery.

## STEP TWO

Separate three sticks of celery from the bunch, and trim them across the bottom.

## STEP FOUR

Ask an adult to cut across the stems to reveal the insides of the stems. What can you see?

## STEP THREE

Place a stick of celery in each glass and leave them for 24 hours.

How do the leaves look after a day?

# LEAVES

Leaves are where plants turn sunlight into food.

Howzat!

## SUNCATCHER

The job of a leaf is to catch sunlight. Sunlight contains energy that plants turn into sugars that they use as food. Leaves are spread out along a plant's stem to catch as much light as possible.

## HIDE AND SEEK

A holly leaf is dark green and spiky. Can you find TWO holly leaves hiding?

## HEY, WHAT AM I?
Which plant's leaves are these?
Answer on page 28.

# SEEING GREEN

Most leaves are green, but they come in lots of different shapes and sizes.

Cheese plant leaves have holes in them, like Swiss cheese!

Clover leaves are heart-shaped.

# EAT YOUR GREENS

Leaves are an important food for many animals, including humans. We eat lettuce leaves and spinach leaves in salads. We use the leaves of herb plants like parsley and basil for flavoring.

# FLOWERS

The flower is where seeds are made.

## PARTS OF A FLOWER

Most plants have flowers. Each part of a flower has a job.

**Petals** are colorful. It is the job of the petals to attract insects.

The job of the **anthers** is to hold **pollen**.

The **style** is topped with a sticky pad called the **stigma**. The stigma receives pollen from other flowers.

The **ovary** is where new **seeds** grow.

## POLLEN SWAP

A plant needs to receive pollen from another flower of the same **species** in order to create new seeds. Visiting insects carry pollen between flowers.

BUZZ
BUZZ

Insects can see colors that humans can't. Some flowers have bull's-eyes for insects in colors that are invisible to us!

Bees see this.

We see this.

### HEY, WHAT AM I?

What are the orange parts of this flower called? Answer on page 28.

## FRUIT

A fruit protects and carries the seeds.

## FLOWER TO FRUIT

Once a flower has received pollen from another flower, the petals fall off. The ovary, where the new seeds are growing, gets bigger and turns into a fruit.

Flowers turn into fruit.

SEEDS INSIDE (!) (!) HANDLE WITH CARE

## SEED CARRIER

A fruit has two jobs. The first job is to protect the seeds as they are growing. The second is to move the seeds away from the plant when they are grown.

Yum!

## JUICY FRUIT

A fruit moves seeds away from the plant with the help of animals. Birds and animals eat tasty fruit with seeds inside. The seeds pass through the animals and are left behind in their droppings.

WOW!

Pomegranate fruits can contain over 1,000 seeds!

## SEED SUCCESS

In the wild, lots of seeds end up somewhere they can't grow. Some fruits contain lots of seeds to make sure at least some will be successful.

# SEEDS AND BULBS

New plants grow from seeds or bulbs.

## SUPER SEEDLINGS

Seeds need water, **oxygen**, and warmth to sprout into a new plant. They shoot little roots downward, and a stem upward. This is called a **seedling**.

A seed is planted.

The seed starts to sprout.

The root and stem start to form.

A seedling is a mini plant.

## GONE WITH THE WIND

Another way that plants spread their seeds is using the wind. A dandelion seed has little feathery wings that catch the wind and carry the seed far away.

dandelion seeds

## BRIGHT BULBS

Some plants, such as daffodils, grow from **bulbs**. Bulbs are like little brown paper packages containing all the food needed to grow a plant.

New bulbs, called **bulblets**, grow on the side of the original bulb, then split off.

### HEY, WHAT AM I?

What can you see in this picture? Answer on page 29.

### HIDE AND SEEK

Can you spot a dandelion seed that has blown somewhere on this page?

# GROW A BULB IN WATER

See how a bulb sprouts into a brand new plant. You'll need:

A glass

A daffodil bulb

A few pebbles

## STEP ONE

Put the pebbles in the bottom of the glass and sit the daffodil bulb on top, pointy side up. Add water to the glass until the water is just below the bottom of the bulb, but the bulb is left dry.

**STEP TWO**

Leave your bulb in a bright spot, but out of direct sunlight, for a few weeks, and watch it grow. Make sure you regularly top up the water to the same level.

What grows first? Roots or shoots?

## TAKE IT FURTHER

If you are very good at waiting and have a garden, you could plant your bulb. Check with your grown-up first, though!

After your daffodil has finished blooming, trim off the leaves and flower from the bulb. Dig a hole in the soil about 6 inches (15 cm) deep, and sprinkle some **fertilizer** inside. Pop the bulb in the hole and cover it up.

In one or two years the daffodil should bloom again. The plant will grow new bulblets under the soil.

# SUNLIGHT

All plants need sunlight to grow.

## HUNGRY FOR SUN

Plants use sunlight, water, and **carbon dioxide** from the air to make food for themselves. This is called **photosynthesis**.

$$\text{☀} + \text{💧} + CO_2 = \text{🌲}$$

## SHADY BUSINESS

Trees try to spread their seeds far and wide. This is because new seedlings need sunlight. They can't grow well in the shade of the **mature** tree.

You're blocking my light!

# LOSING LEAVES

Because there is less sunlight in winter, some trees drop their leaves. These are called **deciduous trees**. Trees that don't drop all their leaves in winter are called **evergreen trees**.

An oak is a deciduous tree.

A pine is an evergreen tree.

## HIDE AND SEEK

Some trees' leaves turn yellow or red before they drop. Can you spot a red maple leaf?

## HEY, WHAT AM I?

What can you see in this picture? Answer on page 29.

# WATER AND WARMTH

Like us, plants need water and warmth to stay healthy.

## NEED A DRINK?

All plants need water, but some plants need more than others. Plants such as banana trees that grow in rainy, tropical areas need lots of water.

## WOW!

Cactus plants can live for several years without water! During rare desert rainstorms, they suck up as much water as possible. They live off the stored water until the next rainstorm.

# SLEEPING SEEDS

During the winter when it is cold, seeds and bulbs don't grow. They wait underground until the weather warms up in the spring.

zzzZ... zzZZ... zzZZ...

## HIDE AND SEEK

Cold, frosty weather can damage or kill small plants and flowers. Can you spot a flower with brown, frost-damaged edges?

### HEY, WHAT AM I?
What can you see in this picture? Answer on page 29.

# PLANT MAZE

Prove that plants grow towards light with this cool maze experiment.

You'll need:

Scissors and some tape

Shoebox and some extra card stock

A potted bean plant

## STEP ONE

Cut two pieces of card stock the same height as the shoebox, but only half as wide as the narrow end of the box. Tape the pieces of card stock inside the box, one on the right and one on the left, dividing the box into thirds.

Ask an adult to help with any cutting.

## STEP TWO

Cut a large hole in one end of the shoebox.

## STEP THREE

Stand the box on its end, and place the well-watered bean plant in the bottom.

## STEP FOUR

Place the lid on the front of the box and tape it up around the edges, so that light can only get in through the hole in the top. After 5 days, take the lid off the front of the box.

How has the plant grown?

# ANSWERS

Page 7

Page 7

**What am I?** I'm a cactus plant

**Hide and Seek** There are 4 daisies hiding

Page 9

Page 12

**Hide and Seek** Holly leaves

**What am I?**
I'm the root hairs on a new plant shoot

Page 15

**What am I?** I'm
lettuce

Page 13

**What am I?** I'm the anther

Page 19

**Hide and Seek**  Dandelion seed

**What am I?**

I'm a plant bulb with a new bulblet growing and splitting off

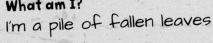

**Hide and Seek**  A red maple leaf

**What am I?**

I'm a pile of fallen leaves

**Hide and Seek** Frost-damaged flower

**What am I?**

I'm bananas on a banana tree

# GLOSSARY

**anther** the part of the flower that holds the pollen

**bulb** a rounded, fleshy part that some types of plant sprout from

**bulblet** a new bulb that starts to grow from the side of another bulb

**carbon dioxide** one of the invisible gases that make up the air, also written as $CO_2$

**deciduous tree** a tree that loses all its leaves in winter

**evergreen tree** a tree that keeps its leaves in winter

**fertilizer** stuff that is added to soil to give nutrients to plants

**flower** the part of the plant where new seeds are made

**flowering plant** a plant that grows flowers

**leaf** the part of the plant that captures sunlight

**mature** fully grown

**nonflowering plant** a plant that does not grow flowers

**nutrients** substances needed for healthy growth

**ovary** the part of the flower where new seeds develop

**oxygen** a gas that is in the air

**petal** the colorful parts of the flower that attract insects

**photosynthesis** a process that plants use to make food from sunlight, water, and the air

**pollen** the dust that flowers swap in order to make new seeds

**root** the part of the plant that grows underground

**seed** the part of the plant that grows into a new plant

**seedling** a seed that has sprouted but has not fully grown

**species** a specific type of plant or animal

**stem** the part of the plant that holds up the leaves and flowers

**stigma** a sticky pad that receives pollen from other plants

**style** a tube that holds up the stigma

**trunk** the woody stem of a tree

# FURTHER INFORMATION

## Books

Gibbs, Maddie. *Let's Find Out! Plants: Types of Plants*. New York, NY: Britannica Educational Publishing, 2019.

Long, Erin. *Spotlight on Ecology and Life Science: Plants and Their Environments*. New York, NY: PowerKids Press, 2017.

Royston, Angela. *Test Your Science Skills: What Do You Know About Plants?* New York, NY: PowerKids Press, 2018.

## Websites

### Brain Pop

*www.brainpop.com/science/diversityoflife/seedplants/*

### Science for Kids

*www.scienceforkidsclub.com/plants.html*

### Science Kids

*www.sciencekids.co.nz/plants.html*

**Publisher's note to educators and parents:** Our editors have carefully reviewed these websites to ensure that they are suitable for students. Many websites change frequently, however, and we cannot guarantee that a site's future contents will continue to meet our high standards of quality and educational value. Be advised that students should be closely supervised whenever they access the Internet.

# INDEX